THE US CABINET

THE PRESIDENT'S TOP ADVISORS

GOVERNMENT LESSONS FOR KIDS
CHILDREN'S GOVERNMENT BOOKS

In this book, we're going to talk about the United States Cabinet. So, let's get right to it!

What Is the United States Cabinet?

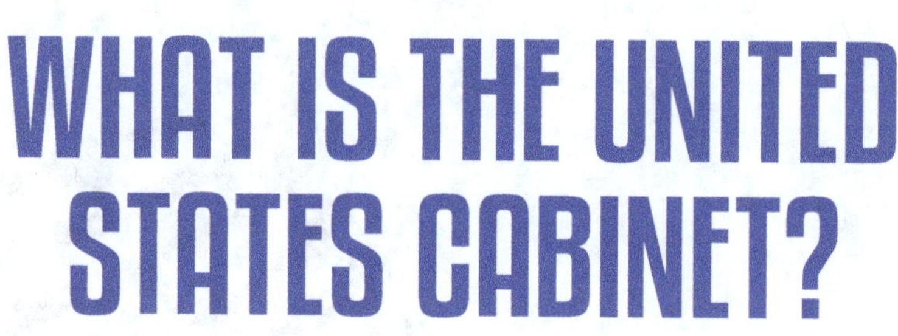

The President needs advisors to help him or her make decisions and to run the different departments of the government. The top advisors assisting the President in the day-to-day operations are called the Cabinet.

PRESIDENT NIXON WITH HIS
FIRST TERM CABINET

JAMES MADISON

Founding Father James Madison first called this important group of advisors "The Cabinet" after the Italian word "cabinetto," which means a small private room. Today, the President's Cabinet consists of:

- ★ The Vice President
- ★ The Attorney General, who is the head of the Justice Department
- ★ The 14 Secretaries of the other departments

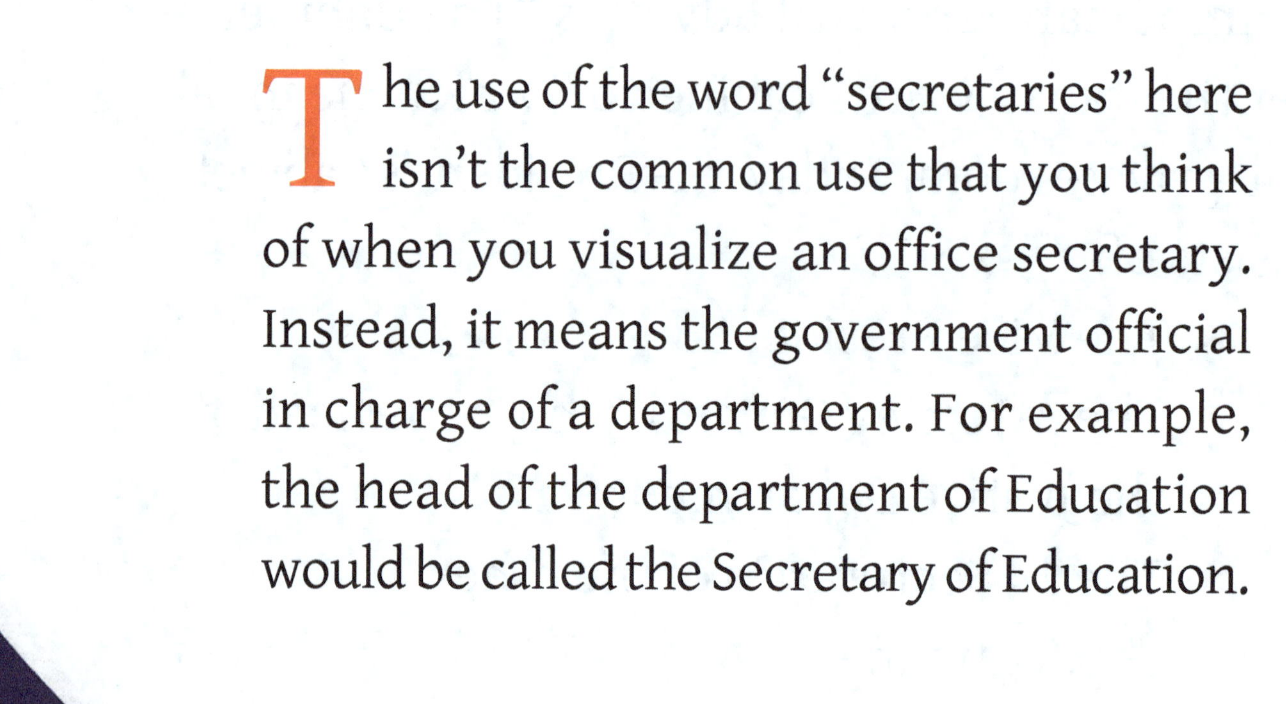

The use of the word "secretaries" here isn't the common use that you think of when you visualize an office secretary. Instead, it means the government official in charge of a department. For example, the head of the department of Education would be called the Secretary of Education.

BETSY DEVOS
SECRETARY OF EDUCATION, 2017

The members of the Cabinet are selected by the President. They must be confirmed by the Senate. If the President is displeased with a member of the Cabinet, that individual can be removed from office at any time.

The members of the Cabinet are very influential and each of the departments they manage is critical to the running of the United States.

GEORGE WASHINGTON PRESIDING
AT THE CONVENTION OF 1787

The very first Cabinet was the one selected by the first United States President, George Washington. At that time, the Cabinet was much smaller. It was only four advisors. The members of the first Cabinet were:

- ★ Thomas Jefferson, who was the Secretary of State
- ★ Alexander Hamilton, who was the Secretary of the Treasury
- ★ Henry Knox, who was the Secretary of War
- ★ Edmund Randolph, who was the Attorney General

DEPARTMENT OF AGRICULTURE SEAL

WHAT ARE THE EXECUTIVE DEPARTMENTS OF THE CABINET?

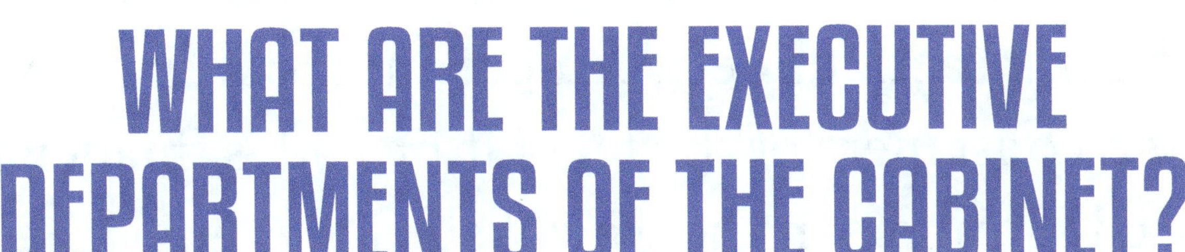

There are 15 different executive departments.

THE DEPARTMENT OF AGRICULTURE

This department was established in 1862 and it oversees the production of all farming and agricultural products in the United States.

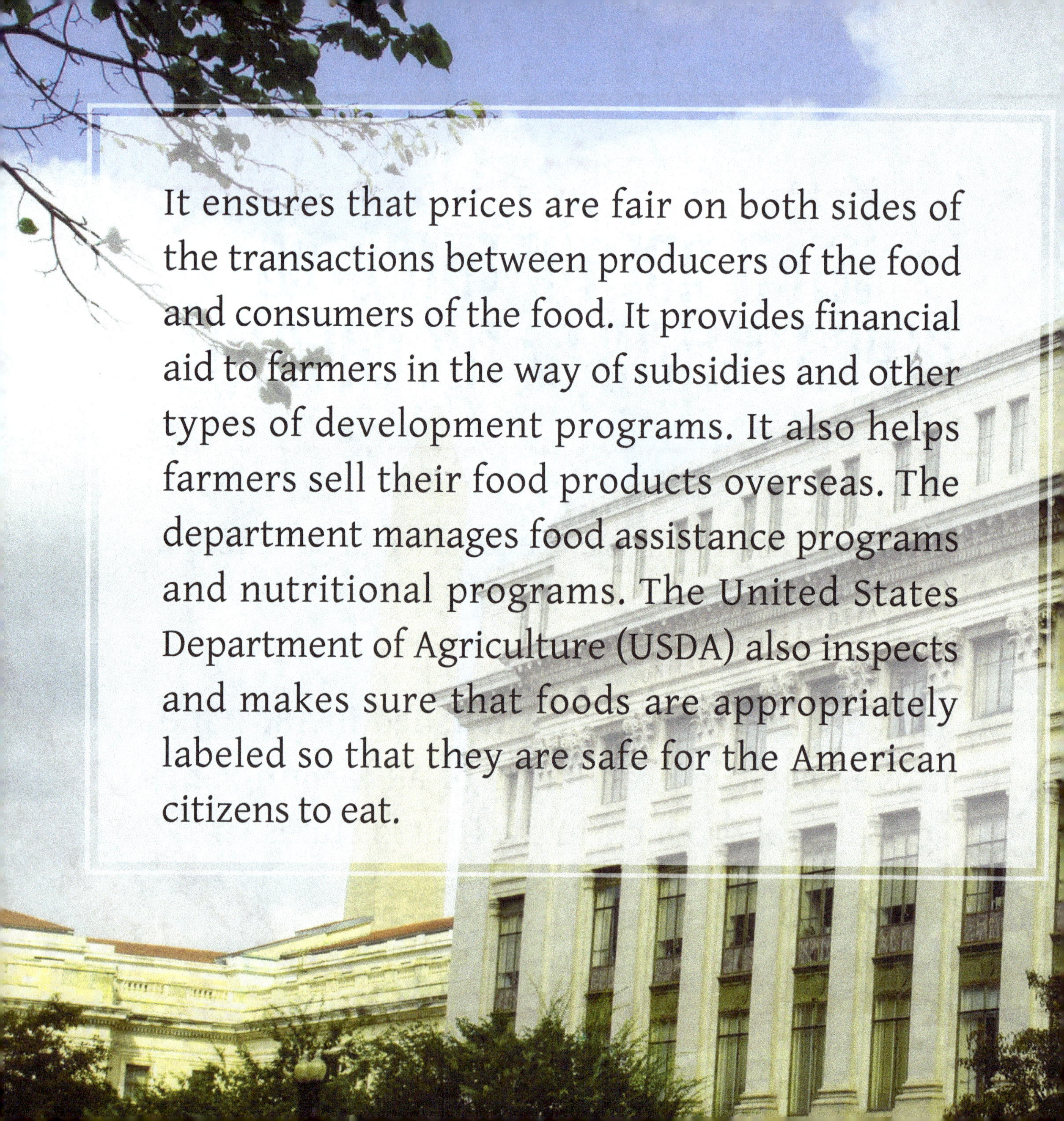

It ensures that prices are fair on both sides of the transactions between producers of the food and consumers of the food. It provides financial aid to farmers in the way of subsidies and other types of development programs. It also helps farmers sell their food products overseas. The department manages food assistance programs and nutritional programs. The United States Department of Agriculture (USDA) also inspects and makes sure that foods are appropriately labeled so that they are safe for the American citizens to eat.

DEPARTMENT OF AGRICULTURE BUILDING

This department was established in 1903 and it promotes trade between the United States and other countries around the world. It's also responsible for ensuring the country has a healthy economy and that the United States moves forward in technological advancement. It works to make certain that the

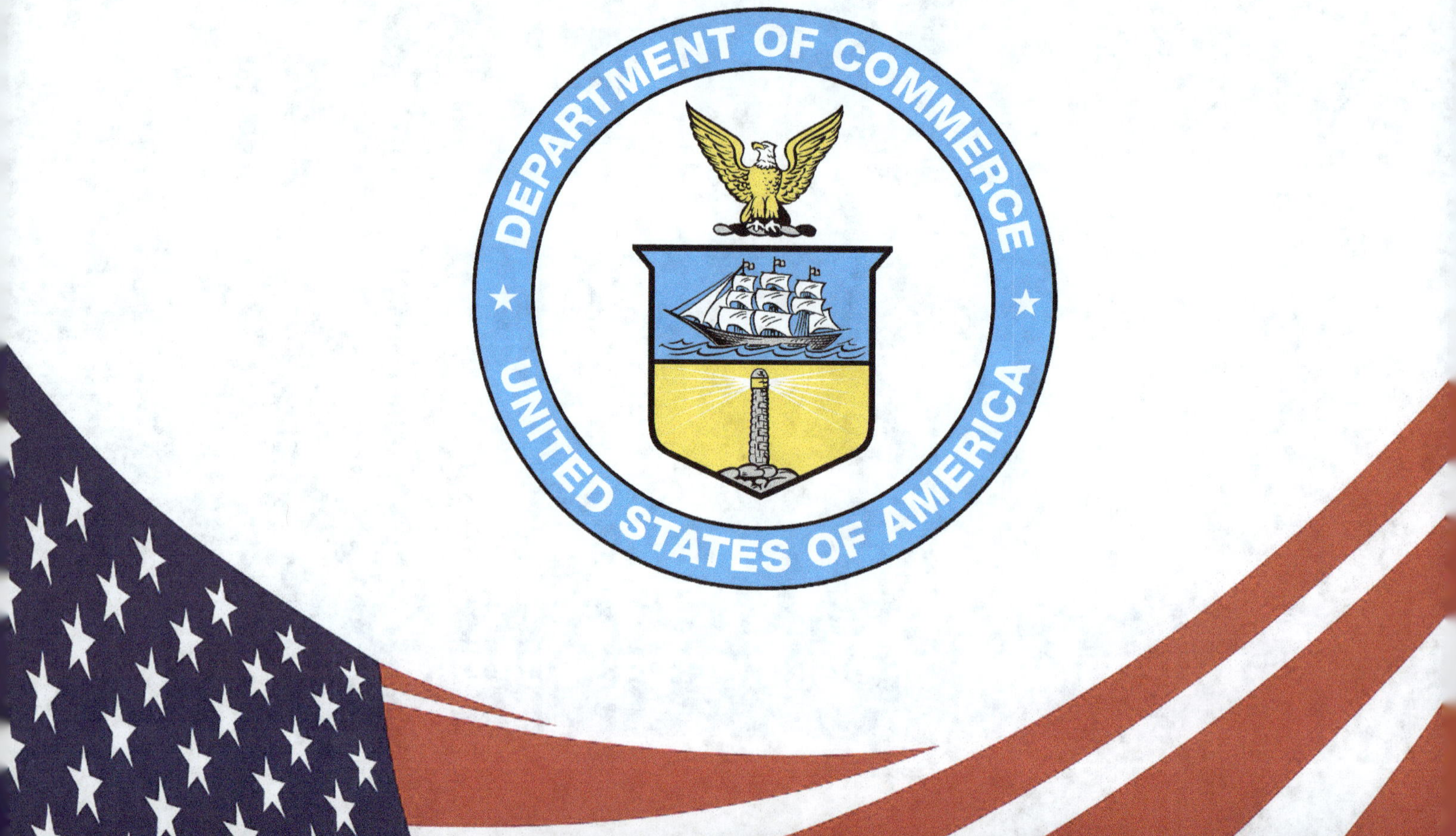

US has a competitive advantage in markets around the world and polices unfair trade practices between foreign countries and the United States. It also collects important statistics for government planners.

THE DEPARTMENT OF DEFENSE

The Department of Defense (DOD) was established in 1947 and it manages all issues related to the military security of the United States. It directs the Army on land, the Navy on the sea, and the Air Force in the air. It also directs the Marine Corps, the Joint Chiefs of Staff, and other specialized combat missions. The DOD has nonmilitary responsibilities as well, such as flood control and the safe management of reserves of oil and other ocean resources.

DEPARTMENT OF DEFENSE
UNITED STATES OF AMERICA

DEPARTMENT OF EDUCATION
UNITED STATES OF AMERICA

THE DEPARTMENT OF EDUCATION

Established in 1979, the Department of Education took over the specialized management of programs related to education that were previously managed by other agencies. It administers over 150 different United States government education programs including training for migrant workers, administration of loans for students, special career education programs, and programs designed for disabled people.

THE DEPARTMENT OF ENERGY

Established in 1977, when the country was having an energy crisis, this department is in charge of energy problems. It manages the research as well as the development of new technologies for creating energy.

It's also in charge of the conservation of energy as well as the uses for nuclear energy, both by civilians and by the military. It sets important standards to help reduce the harmful polluting effects from the use of different forms of energy.

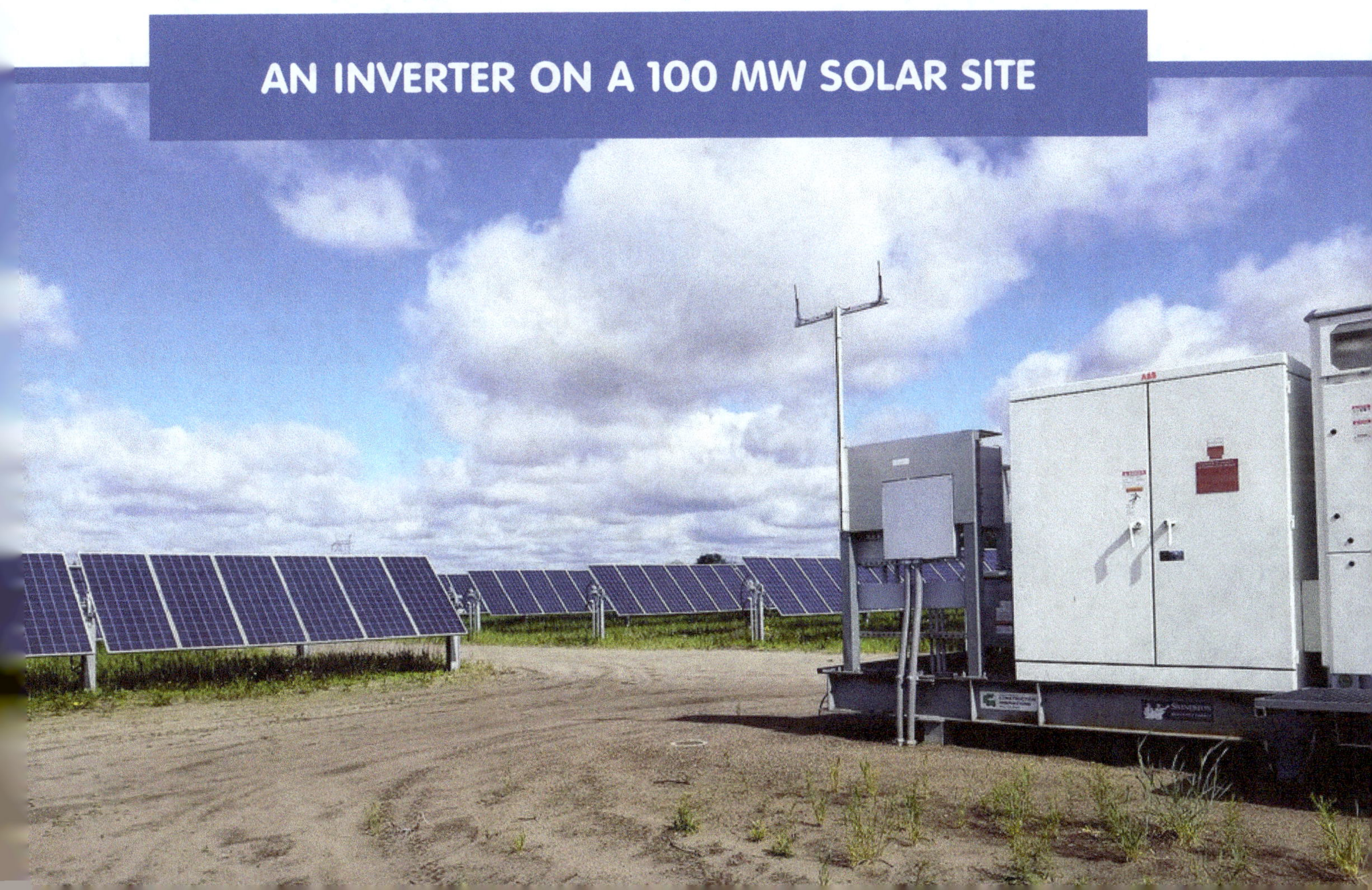

THE DEPARTMENT OF HEALTH AND HUMAN SERVICES

Established in 1953, this department was originally called the Department of Health, Education, and Welfare, but its name was changed once the Department of Education was established. This department has one of the largest ranges of responsibilities of all the departments.

THE DEPARTMENT OF HEALTH AND HUMAN SERVICES

It manages the Social Security program that pays benefits to people who are retired or disabled. Some of the other programs it manages are:

* Medicare and Medicaid for health benefits
* Social Services for impoverished families and the elderly
* The Public Health Service, which deals with issues of mental wellness and drug abuse
* The Center for Disease Control, which works to manage infectious diseases
* The National Institutes of Health, which conducts research on cancer and other diseases
* The Food and Drug Administration, which makes sure that the food supply and drugs are safe for use

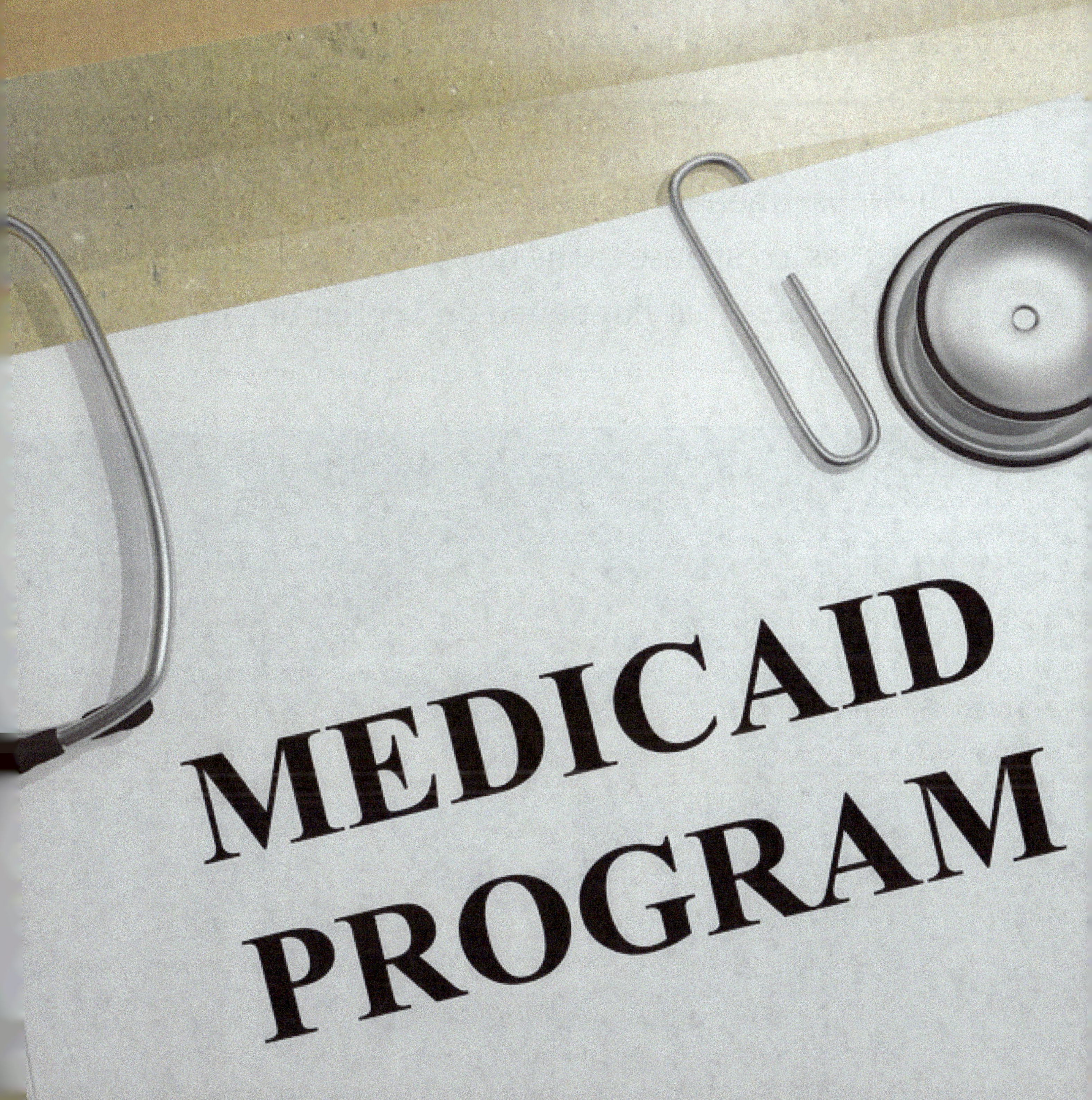

MEDICAID
PROGRAM

The Department of Homeland Security was established in 2003 as a response to the terrorist attacks against the United States that happened on September 11, 2001.

It required a tremendous amount of reorganization to ensure that all the different agencies had a communication network to share intelligence.

I n total, there are 22 agencies including the Secret Service, the Coast Guard, and the Immigration and Naturalization Service sharing information with

NATIONAL OPERATIONS CENTER (NOC), HOMELEND SECURITY, USA

this department. There are over 170,000 employees involved in this department.

THE DEPARTMENT OF HOUSING AND
URBAN DEVELOPMENT BUILDING

DEPARTMENT
OF
HOUSING
AND
URBAN
DEVELOPMENT

THE DEPARTMENT OF HOUSING AND URBAN DEVELOPMENT

Established in 1965, this department, called HUD for short, is in charge of fair housing laws. It works to promote the development of communities. It helps to ensure that affordable housing as well as subsidies for renters are available to people who have low income.

THE DEPARTMENT OF THE INTERIOR

Established in 1849, the Department of the Interior is in charge of the natural resources and environment of the United States. Some of its components include:
★ The National Park Service, which controls all the national parks and monuments
★ The Fish and Wildlife Service, which manages wildlife refuges and fish hatcheries

E St NW
1800
18 St NW
1000

DEPARTMENT OF THE INTERIOR BUILDING

★ The Bureau of Land Management, which is in charge of protecting the environment for public lands that total in the millions of acres

★ The Bureau of Indian Affairs, which assists Native Americans who live on government reservations

DO NOT
ENTER
ONE
WAY

The Department of the Interior is also in charge of the United States territories such as Guam and the Virgin Islands.

THE DEPARTMENT OF JUSTICE

The Department of Justice is managed by the Attorney General and was established in 1870. It is in charge of all United States district attorneys as well as marshals. The department supervises all federal prisons and gives the President advice regarding petitions for pardoning prisoners.

DEPARTMENT OF JUSTICE
QUI PRO DOMINA JUSTITIA SEQUITUR

THE DEPARTMENT OF JUSTICE BUILDING

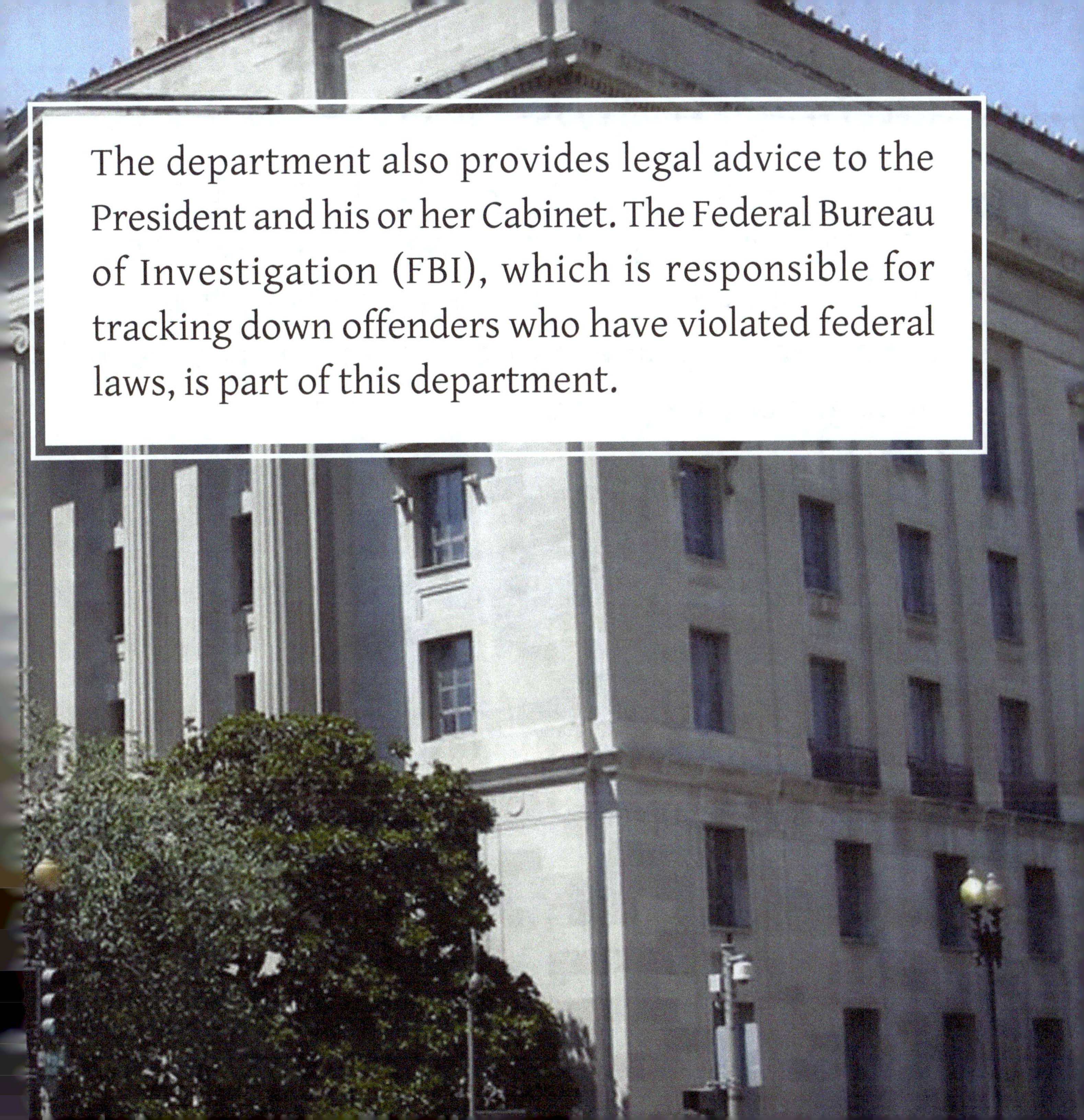

The department also provides legal advice to the President and his or her Cabinet. The Federal Bureau of Investigation (FBI), which is responsible for tracking down offenders who have violated federal laws, is part of this department.

THE DEPARTMENT OF LABOR

The Department of Labor was established in 1913 and its major role is to protect the rights of United States workers as well as their working conditions. It assists in promoting good working relationships between management and labor.

FRANCES PERKINS
UNITED STATES
DEPARTMENT OF LABOR

THE DEPARTMENT OF STATE

Established in 1789, the Department of State provides advice to the President on issues of foreign policy and helps to maintain good relations between other countries around the world and the United States.

It also works to negotiate treaties with other nations and represents the US in meetings at the United Nations. It supervises overseas embassies and consulates.

THE DEPARTMENT OF TRANSPORTATION

The Department of Transportation was established in 1966 and is responsible for setting the United States policies for transportation. Highway planning and construction, mass transit, and railroads are all areas managed by the DOT.

The department is also responsible for the safety of waterways, highways, and pipelines for oil and gas. It supervises the Coast Guard as well.

THE DEPARTMENT OF TREASURY BUILDING

THE DEPARTMENT OF THE TREASURY

One of the oldest departments, the Department of the Treasury was established in 1789. It provides reports to the President regarding the state of the economy. It also regulates the sale of alcohol as well as firearms. It supervises the printing of United States stamps for the postal service. It is in charge of the Secret Service and the Internal Revenue Service.

This department, established in 1989, replaced the former department that was called the Veterans Administration. It is in charge of the health of war veterans as well as their benefits. It offers pensions, home loans, and compensation for those who were disabled when they were part of the military.

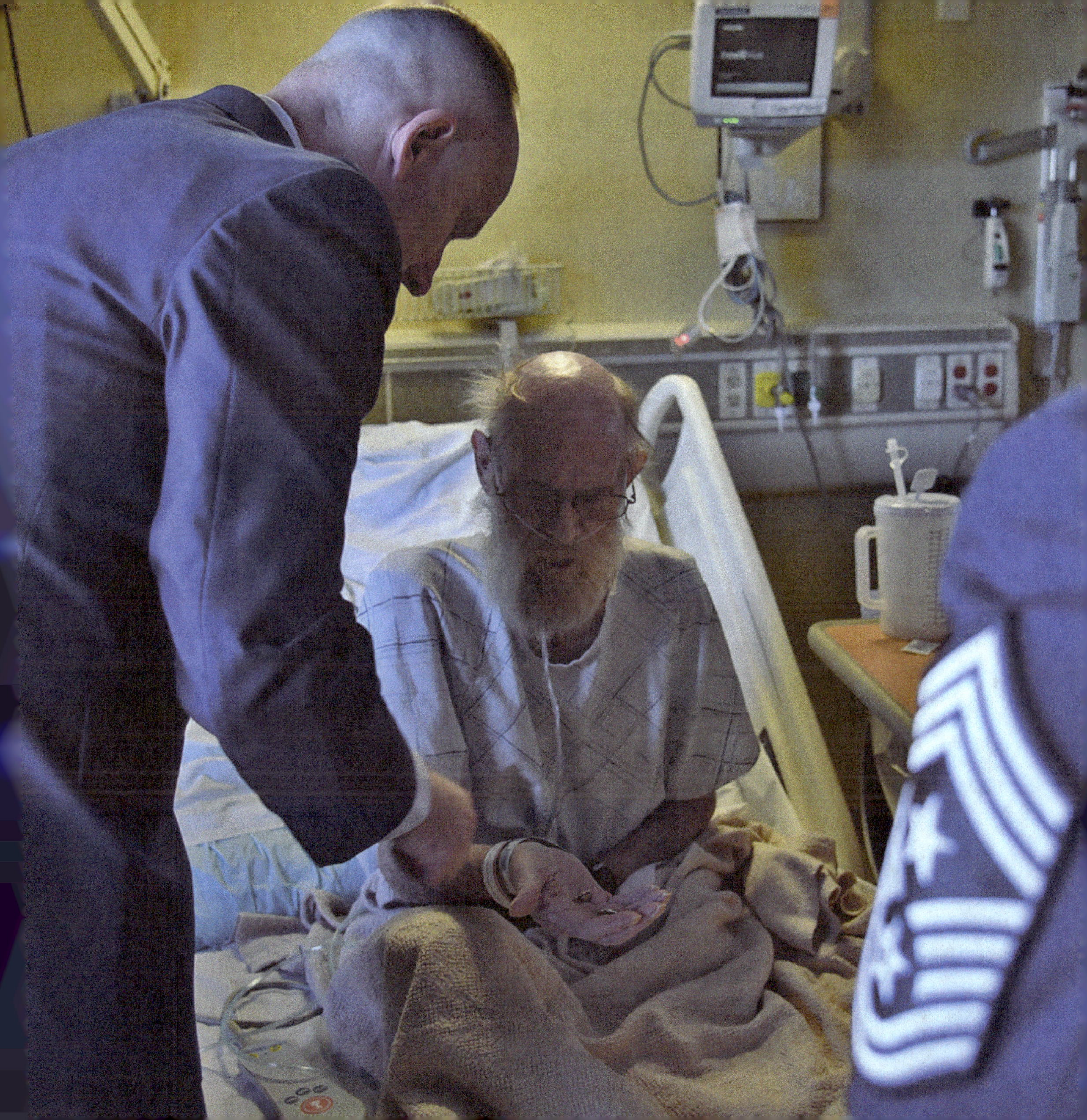

PRESIDENT OBAMA CABINET MEETING 2009

THE PRESIDENT'S ADVISORS

The United States Cabinet consists of 16 influential individuals who advise the President on important domestic and foreign policies. They also run their different departments, which are all critical to the smooth management of the government.

The Vice President, the Attorney General, who is the head of the Justice Department, and 14 other heads of departments make up the President's Cabinet. The other heads of departments are called Secretaries. So, the head of the Department of Education would be called the Secretary of Education.

REAGAN-THATCHER CABINET TALKS

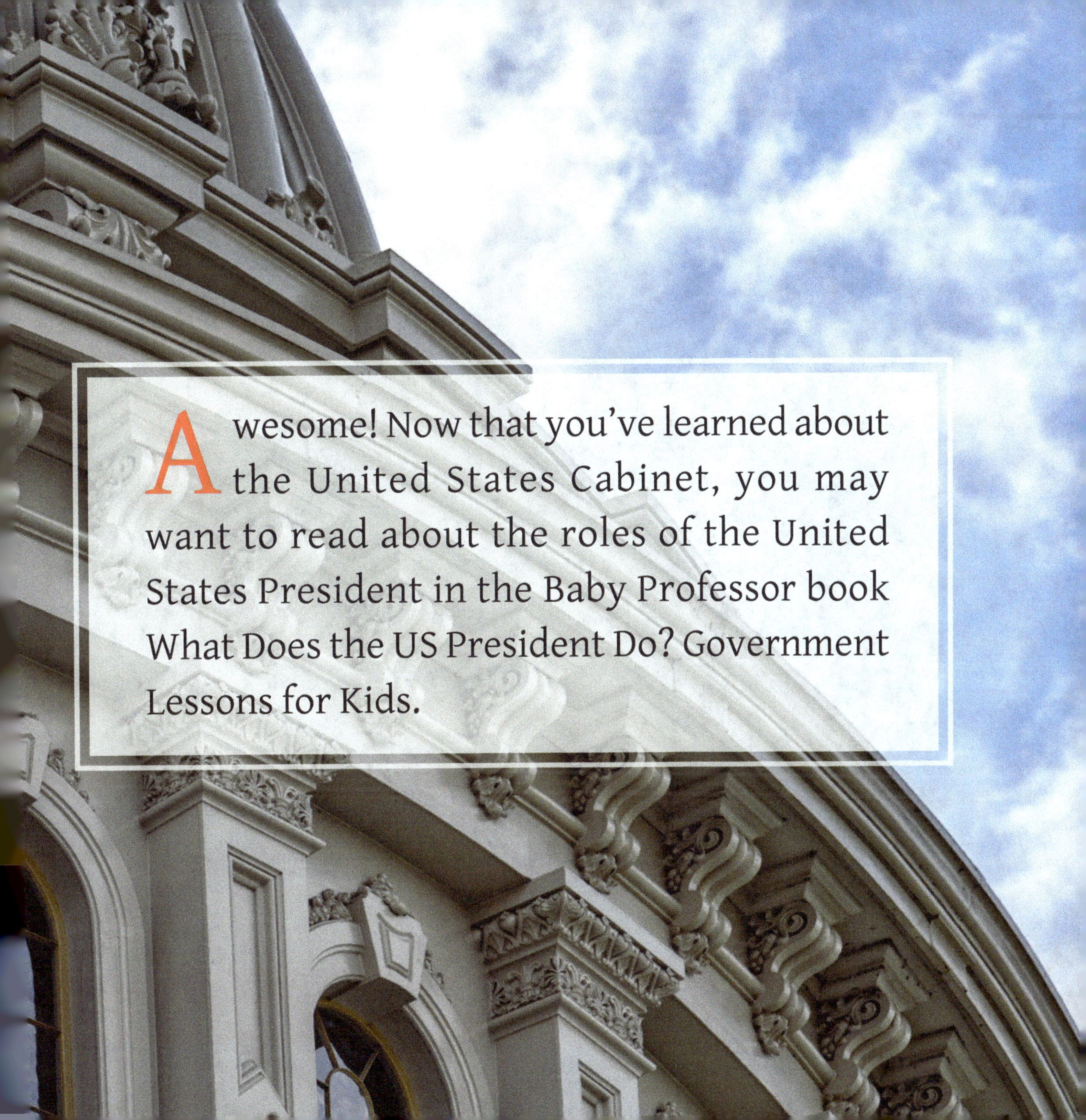

Awesome! Now that you've learned about the United States Cabinet, you may want to read about the roles of the United States President in the Baby Professor book *What Does the US President Do? Government Lessons for Kids.*

Visit

www.BabyProfessorBooks.com

to download Free Baby Professor eBooks
and view our catalog of new and exciting
Children's Books